# POETIC JUSTICE

*VOLUME 2 || 2016*

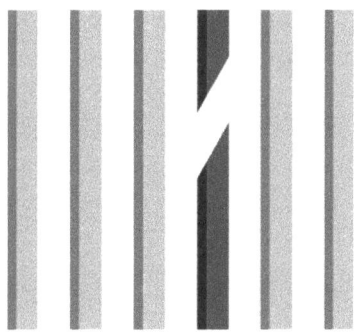

# POETIC JUSTICE

### COMPILED AND EDITED BY
Poetic Justice Inc.

### POETRY BY
Women at David L. Moss Criminal Justice Center
and Mabel Bassett Correctional Center

### PHOTOGRAPHY BY
Hans Kleinschmidt

### GRAPHIC DESIGN & TYPE BY
Colten Sikes

### LOGO DESIGN BY
Jonathan Heckman

### POETIC JUSTICE WOULD LIKE TO THANK
Sheri Curry, Sgt. Stacie Holloway, the officers at David L. Moss Criminal Justice Center and Mabel Bassett Correctional Center, Lauren Zuniga, all those who have donated to Poetic Justice, and the hundreds of women who bravely shared these stories.

### ATTRIBUTIONS
Epistolary poems inspired by Lauren Zuniga's "Dear Lauren Barry."
What It's Like to Be (WILTB) poems inspired by Patricia Smith's
"What It's Like to Be a Black Girl (for Those of You Who Aren't)."

©2016 Poetic Justice Inc.
All Rights Reserved
Printed in the United States of America

ISBN 978-0-692-76140-3

PRAISE FOR
**POETIC JUSTICE**

"What I love about the class is the absolute love and acceptance of us all by the leaders, no matter age, crime, sentence, or ability."

"Before this class, I felt like I was just a number. After, I feel that my voice can be heard and people appreciate what I have to say; they can relate to my struggle as well."

"What I love about this class is that this class gives you a voice. We were able to say whatever that was on our minds, in our heads, and it was acknowledged and appreciated. It was like I mattered."

"I feel confident, triumphant, like a conqueror, and impossible to defeat after finishing this class."

# INTRODUCTION

At the end of Poetic Justice's first class at Mabel Bassett Correctional Center, a student asked me if she could give me a real hug. I knew what she meant by this; she didn't want a fist bump, high five, handshake, or even a hand hug, like the Department of Corrections suggests to volunteers. She wanted a full-on, arms wrapped around neck, inviting human embrace. I accepted and felt this tough, hard shell of a woman turn soft in my holding her. She collapsed a bit, head resting on my shoulder, and I heard her weep "thank you" and "I will miss you" and "this class changed me."

Over two years ago, Poetic Justice began with a simple idea—the idea that words are powerful, even life changing. Two original volunteers, teaching one class to women at David L. Moss Criminal Justice Center (Tulsa County Jail) has grown into twenty volunteers teaching three classes at the Tulsa County Jail and two classes at Mabel Bassett Correctional Center. Now established as an official non-profit organization, Poetic Justice is realizing what once was a simple dream: that poetry can transform a life, even the life of a person in prison.

The United States makes up 5% of the world's population, yet it has 25% of the world's incarcerated people. Oklahoma alone incarcerates more women per capita than any other state in the nation. The thousands of incarcerated women makes the work of Poetic Justice vital.

The poems that fill the remainder of these pages come from 15 different smaller publications from David L. Moss and Mabel Bassett Correctional Center. Their voices cannot be silenced within these pages. I urge you to hear these stories and view these women as the mothers, daughters, sisters, wives, friends, teachers, students, comedians, athletes, and poets that they truly are.

I sometimes wonder if others will care about the stories from these women as much as I have grown to. I question if people will simply shrug their shoulders or look the other way when I tell them about Poetic Justice's mission: to humanize the incarcerated and let the voiceless have voice again. Then I remind myself that we are all, after all, human. We are all skin and bone and blood. We are each telling and writing our stories every day. They each deserve to be heard.

-Hanna Al-Jibouri
Poetic Justice volunteer

## TABLE of CONTENTS
*DAVID L MOSS CRIMINAL JUSTICE CENTER*

| | |
|---|---|
| Preface | 1 |
| 120048 | 2 |
| I Broke Myself Down | 3 |
| 12 Days of Christmas | 5 |
| Loneliness, Keep it Pushing | 6 |
| Love | 7 |
| Respect the Poet | 8 |
| Meth & Me | 10 |
| Rage | 11 |
| Number | 12 |
| Where Are You | 13 |
| Ode to Seeing my Kids | 14 |
| What it's Like to be a Junkie all Alone | 15 |
| When You Left Before Dawn | 17 |
| A Beautiful Tree with No Leaves | 18 |
| Her Ring | 19 |
| Orange is the New Pink | 20 |
| Retribution/Restitution | 22 |
| The Demon Returned | 23 |
| Letter to my Only Daughter | 24 |
| Say it with Butterflies in Your Stomach | 25 |
| I'm a Criminal | 26-27 |
| Love | 29 |

**TABLE of CONTENTS**
*MABEL BASSET CORRECTIONAL CENTER*

| | |
|---|---|
| Preface | 31 |
| We Speak Each Other | 33 |
| Ode to Merciful Judge | 34 |
| Other Side | 35 |
| No Safe Place | 36-37 |
| Dear Broken Generational Curse | 38-39 |
| Granny | 40 |
| The Hurt in my Heart | 41 |
| The Great Escape | 42 |
| Ode to Underwire Bras | 43 |
| Black Queen | 44 |
| Monograph | 45 |
| Farmhouse Future | 46 |
| Dear Labelle | 47 |
| Mama's Arms | 48 |
| Daddy's House | 49 |
| What it's Like to be a Judged Woman | 50 |
| Do You Know what Grief is? | 51 |
| In My Son's Name | 52-53 |
| What You'll Find 5 Year-Old Tasha Doing in her Toybox | 54 |
| What You Find in my Safe Place | 55 |
| Ode to Geese | 56 |
| My Grandmother's Sheetcake | 57 |
| What it's Like to be Me (For Those of You Who Aren't) | 58-59 |
| What it's Like to be an Alcoholic Mom | 60 |
| I Can Hear | 61 |
| What it's Like to be a Caterpillar | 62 |
| Dear Isabel | 63 |
| Ode to Perfume | 64 |
| What it's Like to be a One Legged Wonder | 65 |
| When my Little Sister Asks | 66-67 |
| Yet | 68-69 |

# POEMS from DAVID L. MOSS CRIMINAL JUSTICE CENTER

## PREFACE

David L. Moss Criminal Justice Center or the Tulsa County Jail is a transition place for those who are incarcerated there. It is the first place someone goes if they are arrested; then, they wait for trial, release, deportation, rehab or prison. The women there (300+) may only be there a few hours or days until they make bail. But many of the women are there for months and even years as they await trial and sentencing. They never go outside—other than for a court appearance. They live their lives in a shifting turmoil of confusion, fear, anticipation, dread, and regret.

Our classes are in the housing units or "pods" where the women spend 24 hours a day. We sit in a utility room within the pod on plastic chairs in a circle. There are no desks or tables and we bring paper, pencils, and notebook paper with us. As the women sit and write, it is utterly silent in the room. The pod fades away, the walls fade away and something almost sacred happens as the women pour out their feelings on the page. When the voiceless find their voice, self-worth, empowerment, and hope follow.

These poems reflect the heart of the experience of being an incarcerated woman at the Tulsa County Jail. The writing is raw, unfiltered, honest, and eloquent.

Note: While the news media has been allowed to take pictures of our classes there, we only have the initials of the women who wrote the poetry.

## 1204800

My first mess-up.
My second domestic A&B
Zero visits.
Fourth time this year
I have been to jail.
Zero times I have had commissary.
Zero times people answered the phone.
Lord, I am tired of pushing in
1-2-0-4-8-0-0 only to hear,
"Call refused."

-Q.B.

## I BROKE MYSELF DOWN

Falling sideways through reality,
I never wanted to occupy again.
I push these thoughts away,
But not his hands or his hateful words.
We will both know I'll be calling again.

-B.P.

## 12 DAYS OF CHRISTMAS

12 bitches snoring
11 indigent envelopes
10 clackers clacking
9 bitches whining
8 husbands lying
7 years suspended
6 jailhouse snitches
5 gay… for the stay…
4 canteen queens
3 blind pleas
2 shakedowns
And a contraband Christmas tree
Thanks for the P.T.S.D.!!!

-C.F.

## LONELINESS, KEEP IT PUSHING

Loneliness, damn you.
Look, back off of me.
I'm tired of you,
so now I am getting the nail gun
to pin you to the walls,
Instead of you pinning me.
Damn, loneliness; don't act as if I can't see your presence,
Sneaking up on me.
I know I left you nailed to the walls.
Now get away loneliness
I don't fear you,
For now I have been renewed with God's blessing
Your temptation is dead,
and gone to no longer hurt me anymore
The emptiness of my heart has been filled
With blessed thanksgiving, plus peace and joy.
Now loneliness be gone; I washed my hand
and I'm through.
So get out of my house because I have no need for you anymore.
You thought you could kill me; however, never so because
My God is my strength.
So trying to take my soul is nevermore.

-K.J.

## LOVE

Love is looking into the eyes of my first born.

Love is getting up every two hours feeding my newborn.

Love is waking up at 5:30, getting ready for work
and kids off to daycare.

Love is holding onto them tightly till they fall asleep.

Love is repeating that every day of my life,
and finding peace and being content doing so.

-H.O.

**RESPECT THE POET**

When I first heard this phrase
I thought,
Are they serious?
Surely you jest!
As time passed I began to realize
That respecting the poet goes outside of this
room...
When you respect the poet
You are basically respecting yourself...
When you learn to respect the poet (yourself),
It extends out into the community
You begin to respect others,
And they extend the respect factor...
So kudos to poetic justice for "respect the poet"...
This is a learning tool and is an awesome
way to teach us to respect one's space, words, and life
We all think differently and were made different,
So learning to respect the poet is a step
Learning to love oneself...
Continue to "respect the poet" and surely,
You will see a change...
I have!

-L.W.

## METH & ME

What the meth is going on?
I need to numb the pain,
Tune out the problem,
Stay up, just cause I want it.
Man, I can clean my three bedroom house,
garage, detached garage, ½ the size of my
home in less than three hours.
Mmm I'm hungry.
So another line goes down.
I'll eat, I promise.
A perfect meal down the drain.
Come on, let's go out to eat.
Okay, only because I want out of the house.
No, I just want a soda and some cig. I'm good.
It's dark outside and I want to go home.
Nobody told me this meth mess
Would let you feel like a sexy maniac, but
Make you look like the living dead—dark circles under your eyes,
Meth bugs, and skin and bones,
Patches of hair missing.
Smile, oops, I lost a tooth or two.
No it's meth eating them away.
Did you say something? You didn't!
Then who's been talking to me for the past hour?
What's that outside? I have to go see.
Be back later. Love you.

-C.C.

## RAGE

Pacing like a caged lion
Until I'm enjoying this unseen
Rapturous side of my psyche,
Enveloping me, calm and collected.

Riding the thin line between
A red fog of rage and sanity,
Getting that look in my eyes
Eyes locked on target—locked beyond.

Controlled rage is a tool,
A weapon to be used.
Gauging whom to use it against,
Everything is about timing now…
Developing the thousand-yard stare

Five heightened senses now,
awareness on, uneasy edge.
Ready to snap, to reach out and strike my target
Yet ice runs in my veins… still.

Rage—a double edged sword
that can destroy me as well.

-C.M.

**NUMBER**

Came in with a name,
Walk their halls and leave their walls
As an inmate number,
a number.
You find yourself remembering just as quickly,
like a social, birth date, or death date.

-B.N.

**WHERE ARE YOU?**

"Where are you?" is what she says into the phone.
"In a cell just miles away"
Something she wouldn't understand.
In the mind of a two year old, all she knows is mommy is gone.
And all she knows is,
Ask Mommy "Where are you?"
Those four words, so hard to hear when I promised her I'd always be here.
Where did I go wrong to hurt that sweet baby girl that means so much?
When I said I'd always be a great mom.
I hate she has to ask, "Mom, where are you?"

-J.Y.

**ODE TO SEEING MY KIDS**

April 17. 3:30 P.M.
4 kids run- 5'5, 3'2, 4'10, 3'6.
Patter of footsteps. Hugs and kisses.
Laughter, joy, tickling, running, and screaming.
Shouts of my name. Shy faces.
Wanting this moment to never end.
Bright eyes, sad goodbyes.
I hide in the kitchen and pick up toys.
Pick up candy, and bowls from ramen noodles.
Day is over. 8:00 P.M.
Silent cry.
Last vision.
Sad now in orange once again.

-Q.B.

## WHAT IT'S LIKE TO BE A JUNKIE ALL ALONE (FOR THOSE OF YOU WHO AREN'T)

It's waking up alone, drenched in sweat and sick as fuck.
It's having one thing on your mind, your next fix.
It's figuring out what you'll have to do to get it.
It's doing things you don't want to do,
and choking down the vomit as you do it.
It's closing your eyes and imagining
you are somewhere until it's over.
It's your hands shaking as you search for a vein
and sigh of relief when you see the flash of red.
It's sitting back and letting the rush of relief
flood your body and being able to breathe again.
It's washing the stink off your body
and crying to yourself knowing you are all alone.
And knowing this is what you will do again tomorrow.
Praying to God for it end.
Terrified it never will.

-M.A.

## WHEN YOU LEFT BEFORE DAWN

The language held the everyday wonder,
Between fleeing the beginning and running never ending.
The dawn was thick like sparkling jewels of illuminated stitches.
As if to stitch up my inner most being.
Disturbances emanating from within and then, beyond the light
During the nights under the bridge,
I heard a song.
A syllable, a pause, a whistle, a memory on fire, to kill the pain,
Hope streams, I'll never be the same.
Secret to Eternal Life.
As in life, travelers propelled.
Motives, memories, scared quest, a kiss,
Dreams of freedom, yearn for home.
Seek redemption, conquer another.
Fortified, yet open, ambiguous decipher.
Secret map, mysterious flow, journey alone, disappear
Return rehearsed fearful spirit animal.

-N.C.

## A BEAUTIFUL TREE WITH NO LEAVES
## (WHAT IT'S LIKE TO BE A CHILDLESS MOTHER)

It's waking up to light a cigarette left in the ash tray.
And checking my cell phone with missed calls and texts, wyd, wyd, call me back.
I turn over, go back to sleep, nothing important to me…
Beautiful.
Makeup and hair, brushing and fixing yourself for the night to go out.
Casino maybe, win big?
Change my life back to what it was and what I really want!
The struggle for picture money or to find a babysitter for a few hours, those hugs!
I want to wake to my beautiful twin daughters saying,
"Momma! Can we go outside, swimming, I'm hungry," anything!
To hear your voices!
I freeze frame and all I see is your smiles, your caring eyes, telling me,
"Momma, it's ok; we don't need that doll."

Who knew the root of all evil would have saved us?
I needed help, a hand up, not a stomp to my face.
Moving from hotel to hotel after eviction and our car was impounded.
Money, that's all you wanted?
I would give everything and trade it all to do it over
and try harder for that root,
The tree of life
slowly wilting without its limbs, a.k.a. Jasmine and Julianna.

-H.D.

**HER RING**

I always soar through my career as a drug addict.
I would never take from my mother.
Then the day came when getting high was all I could think about.
Two young boys to feed, no money left over,
My mom's jewelry box I saw.
Inside, her mother's ring, the one we had made for her.
All her children's birthstones set in beautiful white gold.
A ring she was so proud of, a ring she loved,
But my love for a twenty dollar sack,
was what the ring she loved so much was going to bring.

-A.R.

## ORANGE IS THE NEW PINK

They say orange is the new pink
Yeah, that makes you rethink.
We're women locked up in jail
The ones dressed up, hair done, cute nails
Girly girls, that's what they call us.
Babes that wear pink—it means we're soft, huh?
No, not at all.

We survive, by any cost.
We roam through the pod, legs crossed like a boss.
Heads high, the broads think we're lost.
How did we get stuck in this detention,
Because we all make mistakes, didn't I mention?
We like our hand bags, makeup, but want our freedom.
Looking at past glams, like did we really ever need 'em?

Princess looking up, and see her Queen is leaving.
Shackled up in a dungeon, but what's the reason?
Orange is the new pink, yeah that's what you think.
Jail is putting on individual lashes, trying not to blink,
Or walking in the highest heels, forever on our feet.
I don't have to explain it, because it is what you think.
Only how you survive is praising the Lord,
Staying out the way, and most importantly
Never turning weak.

Stay strong and fearless, to all my Queens who can hear this.
Orange is the new pink. Just remember this lyric.

-J.C.

## RETRIBUTION/RESTITUTION

I try to live by the code of the West
Because my daddy said that was the best
The first rule in the code always was, pretty is as pretty does.
Treat everyone with kindness and love,
That's the way to get into heaven above.
I strive to this each and every day,
Until someone pushes me the other way.
One afternoon, I blew up, I admit,
But I couldn't take any more of her self-righteous bullshit.
I begged her to tell me it was all a lie,
That she didn't try to harm my kids on the sly.
She looked at me with an evil grin,
And a twinkling eye that betrayed her sin.
So I cut her phone cord and bleached her clothes,
When I really wanted to hit the bitch in the nose.
I filled her sugar jar up with salt,
Ran her car out of gas til it came to a halt.
Dumped her shampoo out in the shower,
Kept her up till ungodly hours
I ran her credit card up with things for the kids
Sold some of her shit to very low bids.
I would have done more, illegal or not,
If only my dumbass hadn't got caught.

-J.C.

**THE DEMON RETURNED**

With a passion, with convenient timing,
With an enticing offer to control the one thing in my power.
I needed this though,
Months of laziness produced an ugly sight,
Now I have nothing but time.
A deep longing for me to feel my ribs,
My spine, my abs
to know I have complete control again.
To feel the pangs of hunger
knowing my appetite cannot control me anymore.
Feeling satisfaction as I count my calories,
Carving my body into a temple, my temple.
Silent satisfaction as my family and friends express concern
While simultaneously hugging me,
and stealing a subtle count of my ribs.
Complete.

-C.M.

## LETTER TO MY ONLY DAUGHTER

Momma love you more than you will ever know.
Momma miss you more than you will ever feel.
Momma need you more than you can ever imagine.
Momma taught you to be prepared for this fucked up world.
Never knew you were really paying attention
and will take my words and advice
and take off running with them.

Remember conversation rule the nation,
Never lay-up bareback and dry pockets.
You can never be re-raised by anyone,
Respect yourself at all times.
Never let a man put his hands on you,
Love is blind but love don't hurt.

-B.N.

## SAY IT WITH BUTTERFLIES IN YOUR STOMACH
*To My Girls*

Girls,
I hope you will or already have forgiven me.
I wish I had the strength to take back the years
I've lost without talking to you.
Maybe you have felt abandoned because
we haven't been able to talk for more than a few years.
But I hope you haven't thought that I haven't cared
or wanted to be there for both of you.

If I could light a candle and pick a rose
each time I thought about you two,
It would probably light up a mountainside
where you can see it from outer space
or eagles could soar and see it from the sky.

I just want you to know and have
the peace of God, and happiness and joy.
I want you to have the love and mercy and the grace of God.
I did not mean to break your hearts.
I hope that life has been good to both of you.
I hope and believe that God has provided you with comfort
and all your spiritual and physical and emotional needs have been met.
Next time we see each other,
let's share some sweet candy (Starbursts) and a smile and hug.

With Love,
Your Momma Rose

-R.T.

## I'M A CRIMINAL

18, walking into Walmart, lookin' fly as fuck,
I have a pocketful of money and a pocketful of drugs
So you know what's up.
Carry myself as a man,
Often labeled as a "stud" or "little boy."
Oh shit, my mama's calling.
I'm not concerned about what she sent me to Walmart to do,
I have no agenda.
Grab the backpack—grab the black Dickies,
Grab the Dickies shirt, stuff that shit, bro.
Phone rings again, damn woman, stop callin'
I'm comin' with your meds, but what you don't know is,
I'm a criminal.
First it was little, petty things like games,
socks, drumsticks, hell whatever I can grab.
I have an addiction to the point where I'm bold about it.
Look at this nice dressed little boy with a girlish smile,
Walkin' around the store,
Flirting with a grown woman, but what they don't know is,

I'm a criminal.
Started at six with my god-sisters.
Now I'm onto bigger things.
Hot checks, cars, I'll even rob your house,
I'll take your woman.
After all, been gay since I was a kid.
Now I'm grown and on my own.
I'm a criminal with a fetish fully for women,
Been mistreated in the past by men,
with the thought that this is me.
Always been told I'll never change.
I'm a criminal, and I run around looking for Love,
Bouncing woman to woman cuz after all I'll never change.
I'm a criminal.
A black girl that carries herself as a boy,
And a criminal that you believe will never change.

Game Over.

-Q.B.

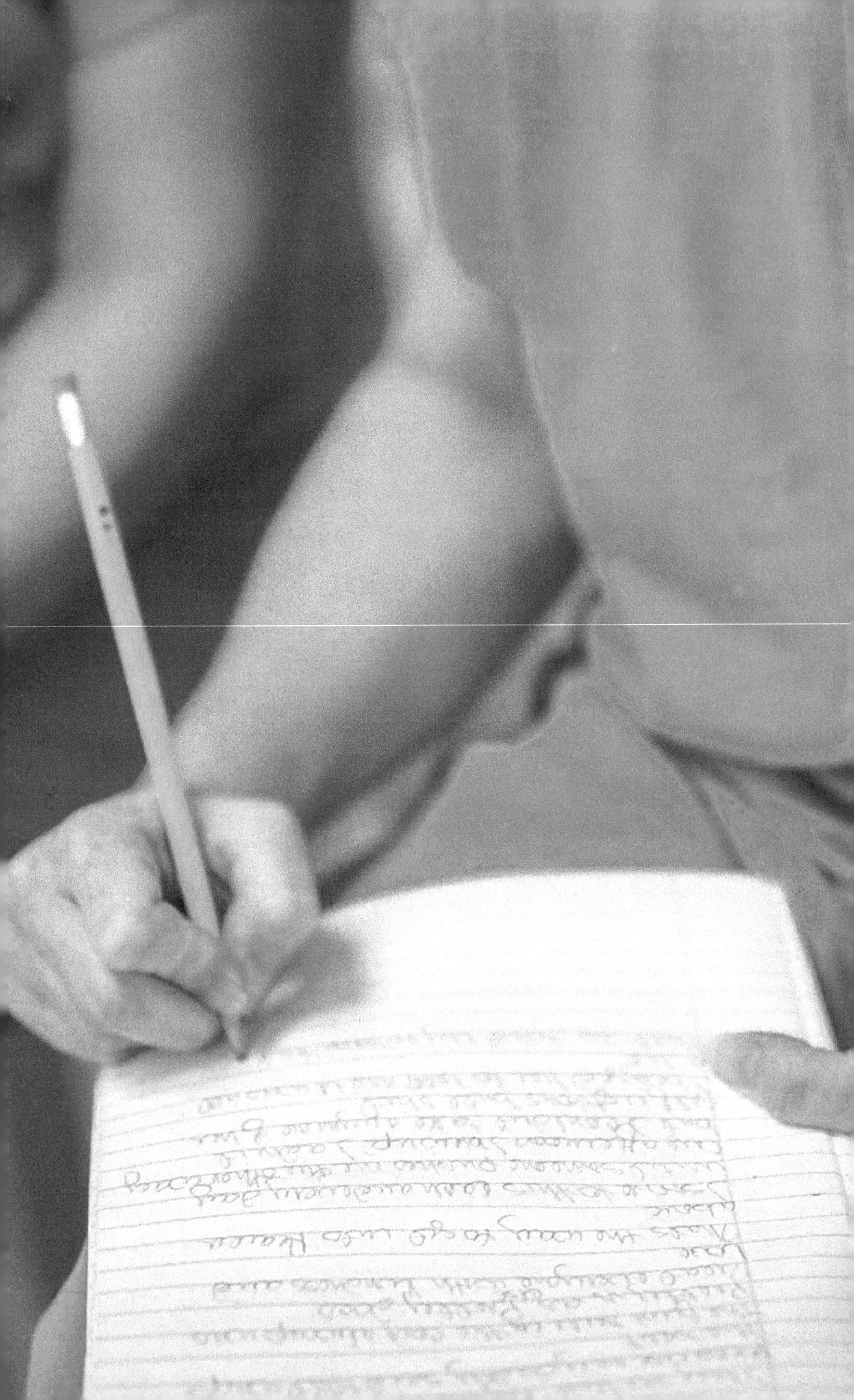

**LOVE**

I have watched it recede
I have reached for it
I have called out to it
And I cried when it vanished.

Some things never come back.

-L.W.

# POEMS from MABEL BASSETT CORRECTIONAL CENTER

## PREFACE

Mabel Bassett Correctional Center is a massive grey prison surrounded by a double razor-wire fence. It is in a remote part of Oklahoma and only fields and a solitary rural cemetery border it. It is Oklahoma's only medium/maximum security prison for women. Built to hold 1,100 women, it currently holds 1,400—113% of capacity.

Poetic Justice classes are held in two classrooms in the prison's chapel. The women sit at tables, have pens and pencils, notebooks, and paper. Many of them have been writing for years and, as a result, our classes there seem more like graduate seminars in a creative writing program than poetry workshops in prison.

These women know what to expect from each day. They know how many times throughout the day they will be counted by officers. They know what the menu at the cafeteria is. They know who they will see, and who they will not see, as they pass hours in the yard. And, they know their sentences; for many women in our classes it is 25 years, for others it is life without parole. One student was sentenced to life without parole when she was 18 and she is now 42 years old. Another only received a 25-year sentence, but she is 60 years old and knows she will never leave prison alive.

These are the women in our classes. They are serious, funny, thoughtful, and wise. They write about their journeys—about remembered places and foods and people that they will never see again. Their writing reflects their struggles to find meaning and life in a place where they have been reduced to drab grey uniforms and a six-digit number. The depth and eloquence of their writing is extraordinary and compelling.

Note: There are no pictures from our classes at Mabel Bassett, but every writer featured in this part of the anthology specifically requested we use their names, and signed releases for us to do so.

## WE SPEAK EACH OTHER

I want my home with the cypress wild
Clinging to the edge of the cliffs
With grief-scrabbled talons,
Roots seizing stone.
The battle to survive is all.
Winds and rain come,
Come hard and swift and relentless.
It's the season for storms.
How does the cypress stand?
How do twisted limbs prevail?

When morning breaks
—and break it shall—
Will home be as I remembered?
Will the cypress ever whisper of me?

-Jax

## ODE TO AN UNMERCIFUL JUDGE

Thank you for using the harshest punishment
That the law allowed at eighteen.
You could have shown me mercy but you
Chose to be unforgiving forever.
My family contrives to write you asking for leniency
But you ignore our prayers, tears, petition, requests.
Through the years I've changed, am now an adult
Who has been rehabilitated over 24 years
There's no more classes, programs for me to take.
Done them all at least three times each.
A lot of my small family has gotten older,
Gone to be with the Lord.
Arthritis has taken hold of their hands, knees.
They can't write, drive to plea for me.
I paid an attorney $3,000 to go see you for me
Only to be told he died on me.

-Lisa Rawlins

## THE OTHER SIDE

As I walk these steps
the steps are getting slower.
As the day goes by I become weaker.
Is my strength failing me?
As my heart beats it skips one or two.
I'm becoming weaker day by day.
As we live without love
the sadness eats at you.
Destroying the inner self
but yet you're still here
fighting the emptiness and pain.
As the walls close in
you fight the fight of no return.
You refused to become a part.
With love there's strength
with strength there is victory
with the victory there's freedom;
so run on that freedom.
On the other side of these walls
is family waiting for you.

-Sharon Smith

**NO SAFE PLACE**

There is no safe place. The only place to be safe is a place where I am alone. I am twelve maybe—before state's custody or after a brief stint at the Frances Willard Home for girls which didn't last long because I ran away. So I am twelve and it's summer. I remember because I am wearing shorts and tennis shoes and no socks but the shorts don't have front pockets and I have a pack of cigarettes in my back pocket. Or maybe the shorts have didn't have pockets and the cigarette is in my shoes. And some matches. One cigarette—it's my last one and a paper book of matches. I am going down by the river.

The Poteau River runs red and muddy over the hill on the backside of my mom and dad's property. I go through the woods and pass the pond where I used to go swimming with Titor before I went to the group home and my dad shot him for biting my brother Sam. I go up the hill and back into the trees which are mainly oak with full green leaves that rustle busily in the slightest breeze. At the top of the hill which stops abruptly, a much steeper, slicker, scarier descent downwards begins. You have to watch out. The upside is all fallen leaves from a hundred years of autumns and rocks with patchy moss the color of bleached verdigris but the downside is slick, hard, bald mud, and the skinny trees with no helpful hand holds.

Their sudden ditches and gullies that pepper the sliding, sidling, stuttering fast progress with half jumps and leaps. Sweating and winded but feeling victorious to have made it to the bottom without having bit it big time on the trip. So here I am. And it's damp. The river is swift, muddy red brown, and I wonder if it's full of leeches or if I'd drown if I jumped in and how I'd get back out. But I don't.

I find a place to sit. There are deer tracks deep in the steep muddy bank and I see a tree growing sideways out of the ground. This is where I sit. The river makes a soft noise. I don't think you could hear it if you weren't alone. Listening for it. The leaves and vines flutter and creak. It's cooler here by the water. I am all sweat and bark and the unnoticeable detritus of trees and dirt. I only smell green. Fecund mud and water and all the things people grew out of. I am my own tribe. I am alone. I take out my tobacco offering to myself and the sharp sulphur of the match stings my nose as the bright burst of ignition stings my eyes. And the acrid wildfire smoke stings my throat and lungs. It tastes like shit. It tastes like heaven.

I smoke and watch something rustling in the brush on the far bank. It is probably an armadillo. And I guess it doesn't know it should be afraid of people because you are only safe when you're alone.

He'll figure it out.
Prey always learns.

-Geneva Phillips

**DEAR BROKEN GENERATIONAL CURSE,**

When you are 33 on the very day of your birth you will be asked to write one of the hardest letters in your life. It will be addressed to the younger you and the things you will say might make you cry and mourn for the loss of your childhood and the incarceration of your adulthood. Here is your letter:

You will be born a quiet baby who has mittens on each hand just to keep your fingers from being bloodied while you sleep. When you are one, just a little guy, you'll have perfected the art of blending into walls, cleaning up blood, and moving while staying really still. You will think this is normal. You will learn how to hide your baby brother when he cries too loud and how to put out a fire when your older brother tries to protect you from the "boogie man." As you grow older you will figure out that if you want to eat you have to learn how to cook. Clean clothes means learning how to wash them, and if you and your two brothers want to go to school you had to get up on your own and get them ready as well. You learn not to talk to people. They ask too many questions. You will not have time for friends so you'll never learn how to have fun or just laugh freely. Because of the secrets you keep buried deep inside, you will become a teenage alcoholic who cuts herself to hide the pain. You will drop out of school to get a job just so you can make sure your brothers have a roof over their heads.

Because you spent your life taking care of your family you will never learn how to have a normal conversation, nor will you feel comfortable looking people in the eyes. You will never gain a sense of self-esteem or self-worth. As time passes and you grow older you'll follow in your mother's footsteps and learn all over again what it takes to truly blend into the walls, how to clean up blood, and move while staying really still. You will always be scared of men and even authority figures.

Anytime attention is drawn to you for any reason you'll do anything and everything to deflect it for fear of repercussions. You will have a permanent red face that others will mistake for anger, but will know it as embarrassment or nervousness because you are easily scared.

When you stand up for yourself and try to leave the one you're with, he will try to take your life, yet you live although it brings you to a place called prison. You learn it's the first time in your life you truly feel safe. And though it will take years and years of struggle you will one day discover that on your 33rd birthday as you sit writing a letter to your younger self that you might actually like the person you are becoming.

P.S. Happy Birthday from the older you.

-D.J. Hopson

## GRANNY

Ever since a child, I've found comfort here
Right in between your arms
Even as an adult, you now still hold me dear
Our bond so tightly formed

No time no distance could keep us apart
You were always where I wanted to be
As an infant we were instantly joined at the heart
My Granny and her favorite—me
I love you, Granny, blessed to have you
The angel here in my life
Without you who knows just what I'd do
You're sharp and steady as a knife.

-Erica Bonner

## THE HURT IN MY HEART

The day I lost everything to a fire
that took my whole world and it
came down on me
because the fire took three of my kids
and I got burnt by trying to save my kids.
But that day everything went upside down
and I had three kids that passed away
and I lost everything that day
that is why my heart hurts bad.

-Stephanie Dunham

## THE GREAT ESCAPE

My daughter calls this place my kingdom of grey.
I was feeling kind of blue as I held my girls last Saturday . . .
Grey walls
Grey clothes
I look around and see grey skies
Grey frogs—Hold up, a grey frog is sitting next to us on the table.
"Hello, little friend. How long ya in for?" I said,
right as my girls noticed the incognito amphibian.
Squeals of delight followed as they proceeded to try and catch "Oshy."
My children could not have been more hilarious if they had tried
it was straight out of a Stooges movie.
A water bottle was quickly commandeered
so that Oshy could have a wet place to sit.
That dang frog treated it just like a hamster ball and rolled all over visitation
Everyone around our table was subject to our hysterical laughter.
At one time, I noticed my oldest writing a number on the bottle
and when I inquired she said, "Duh, Mom. It's his DOC#!"
More laughter.
Well, guys. I'm happy to report that although
my kingdom is still grey, my blues have departed.
And, what pray tell happened to Oshy the tree frog?
Well, Oshy escaped with my kiddos and is now a lovely shade of green.

-Lisa Black

## ODE TO UNDERWIRE BRAS

How I crave your metal wires,
and anyone who doesn't agree are all liars.

I miss your cups and your hooks too,
it's what divides us from the animals in the zoo.
White, black, or even mustard yellow will do.
However, my favorite bra was always baby blue.

For now I'm stuck with the uni-boob deluxe,
it's just one of the things that make me feel like a putz.

I regret that my girls no longer divide,
I truly believe it's even affecting my stride.

I miss you bra, forever and until the end,
and this is only one reason I won't be back again.

-Tasha Roberts

## BLACK QUEEN

Like Lazarus I was dead
Until I picked up a book and read
The history of you, Queen
What you did, what you said
How you lead and spoonfeed
Knowledge to me
Answering my pleas
Even when I couldn't see
The forest for the sea of trees and leaves
Knocking me to my knees
Without blinkin' or thinkin'
Broke down or thinkin'
You picked me up
Saved me from my demise
Helped me rise
Made me realize and recognize all the lies
That I couldn't see with my own eyes
As they were focused on the wrong prize
So no longer out in the fold of the cold
A lost soul, to mold with no goals
Behold a warrior, true
Revised and made new
Caramel through and through
All for you
A strong black woman
In front of you I stand, command,
demand everything on dry land
The seven seas and even the breeze
To freeze, and seize a still scene
Long enough to bow down
To the Black Queen

-Aqueelah Lawton

## MONOGRAPH

The musty funk of dusty peas
Clings to hands hampered by arthritis
And showing their paper-dry age.
I am an old book,
Cover tattooed and adventure-scarred,
Insides stuffed with philosophies and histories
No one cares to read anymore.
Dog-ears mark favorite spots,
Pressed flowers tint lovers' memories,
And tear stain etch holes
Where laughter left us fit to burst.
I am lonely, here on this shelf,
My dear,
I miss your eyes upon me.

-Jax

## FARMHOUSE FUTURE

Two years, eight months
All I think about is the Farmhouse
"Fuller Farmhouse,"
Renamed "Peaceful Acres."
My mother's decision
I love it.
It's so close now, my thoughts are consumed
All I have to do is close my eyes
I can smell the fried okra sizzling in oil
(being cooked in my grandmother's seasoned iron skillet)
The creaking screen door opening up
Letting in a hint of cow shit,
Mixed with the sweetness of honeysuckle
(I wonder where that's growing?)
My favorite spot engrained in my thought
Is sitting on the front porch swing
There I'll sit, slowly swinging back and forth.
Sweet tea, birds chirping, chicken scratches
Oops, there went that slithering snake,
I'll leave him be.
Sunset filling the sky with a rainbow of deep, rich colors
There's so much I love
I inhale, exhale, ooooh, it just got better.
My boys Jared and Celcy just called out
"Hey Mom, what's for dinner?"
Almost there!

-Tammy Brooks

**DEAR LABELLE,**

Girl you hold unforgiveness like a newborn baby making it complicated to move into the ideal life. Strife . . . dwelling in the presence of darkness. What's insane is that the use of it has created a young woman full of rage. Dangerous . . . quiet, kept in as you walk. Becoming a misogynist that barely takes. You buried her, the one who He began . . . She's still breathing . . .Let her up, it's okay keep going, be you, don't allow anyone to tell you how to be you. You . . .are . . .beautiful, a masterpiece made by the Master. Never attempt to believe that you were made for disaster. Your imperfections are to shape your future in each and every section. Fear ain't real, close your eyes if you have to. Powerful suicide is not an option . . .Covered by grace you do mean something. Peace be still. I speak blessings over your being . . .You're more than what you see and even what you've been told. This is a truth that is not to be sold.

Love,

-Sharee Asberry

## MOMMA'S ARMS

Walking up the steps to the porch she was there.
I had called.
A warning of need cellular style.
My mother stood in the doorway arms open.
I walked to her, not a word spoken.
I couldn't speak.
A child, even a young adult, doesn't have to.
She didn't flinch from the blood, but drew me closer.
The tears fell silently.
I crumbled,
a jigsaw in her arms of steel.
Her sense of floral enveloped me
while her fingers laced my hair.
Her heartbeat quickened yet never betrayed
the calm nor the safety
I needed in her arms the night girl I never knew
shot herself and I couldn't save her,
yet her blood stained my memory for life
despite the safety of momma's arms.

-Kelly Romo

## DADDY'S HOUSE

      Tornados can't touch me when I'm curled up safe in Daddy's house. The weatherman tries to get me concerned, but I just smile. I was told since I was five that my father used twenty nails to every one that a normal person would use. He did this to keep me safe. To keep me protected. I laugh at the wall clouds from my porch. I can smell the rain in the air as well as Momma's sheet cake in the oven . . .I feel so safe. I feel so bold. I taunt the storm knowing it can't touch me.

Ah, my poor neighbors.

-Lisa Black

## WHAT IT IS LIKE TO BE A JUDGED WOMAN

Ever walked a mile in these worn and tattered shoes?
You wouldn't desire to.
But how easy is it to judge something you know nothing about.
What gives you the right?
What makes you think you can?
Each day waking inside this dark mind,
Tormented by twisted barbwire thoughts,
Trapped like a caged animal.
Freedom wasn't snatched by the system
I managed to lock my own damn self up!
Label me all you want
But I'll never pay attention.
I'm capable of passing judgement all on my own.
Don't need any help from you!
But thanks anyway
If you ever do want to know
Who I really am
You will have to know
What it's like to be . . .a judged woman.
Wait . . .
I think you do.

-Tammy Brooks

## DO YOU KNOW WHAT GRIEF IS?

Well, I met grief at your funeral. He was wearing basketball shorts, a tank top, and a pair of tennis shoes, that hot, hot day in July. Smoking a joint by himself off in the distance; he put it out just as a funeral director rushed over.

Grief was sexy, not crying, just being himself without apology. I knew he would be staying at my house that night. We got high and drunk and then stayed up all night crying, reminiscing about you, laughing, holding each other's hair back while we puked. We smoked a lot of cigarettes on the porch that night.

I thought it would be a one-night thing, but now grief knew where I lived. He started showing up at my door in the evenings, and sometimes first thing in the morning, too. He begged me to stay home from work. We would just get high and drunk and yell at no one in particular, would trip and fall countless times on the way home. We would stay up for days watching movies and avoiding people.

My friends weren't crazy about him. My sister told me he would eventually have to leave. We fought a lot. I got tired of his constant presence, always right next to me, even when I peed. Sometimes I would ignore him for days, but he was patient, sitting in the corner, waving whenever I looked in his direction.

-Pamela Belk

## IN MY SON'S NAME
*Tamir Rice, Charles Petit, Quintonio Legrier, Trayvon Martin, countless others . . .*

We live in a country where it is clearly evidenced
By history and legal precedent
That it is acceptable to murder certain folk.
Just throw that monkey off the boat.
Police officers don't receive so much as a chiding
For filling a so called Black preteen's chest full of sizzling death.

In my little world, I hear, "Serves him right" or
"That's what he gets for running from the police" or
"What's he doing wearing a hoodie in that neighborhood anyway?"
"You shouldn't speak out, Olympia. They deserved it."

This, from people who don't know what it's like to
have a black man for a son in America and lose him.

So, I (a so-called "black woman") don't talk a lot.
I do honestly believe it's a poison of the heart.
I'd rather write.
In the meantime, while I attempt to hone my craft,
I give birth to nations, then educate them.
So, why shouldn't I shout?

I SCREAM for all my murdered sons and daughters, no matter what race they ran.
I WAIL for my fellow mothers
I YELL to release the banshee of my spirit to invoke and provoke her:

"Haunt and serve justice to all robbers of child souls, those who hover above the law.
For their slain victims' blood is now our only salve drying caked on their hands.
Our wombs are tired, cringing, crying.
So redeem the stolen souls of mine and my sisters' progeny."

And feel the earthquake in my surname's sake
where there never before has been
storming out of normal
like sleet in the Sahara.
Two more go down in Chicago.
But you don't know because
innocents massacred is the background music of Americana.

I'll stand alone to cry out "injustice" if I must for our children.
Black lives don't matter. That's the problem. I can and I will only spit truths.
Miss me with catchy slogans of unreal circumstances chanted in calm protest
just to blow off steam, I'd rather scream.
A black unmother's voice is too powerful to merely mutter the obvious or the untrue.
I'll scream 'til I turn blue.
For my maimed mahogany grandmother's soul to reach peace and paradise.
Yell for our bullet-flayed sunfavored neighbor's soul!
Because God forbid yours is next.
SCREAM for our lives, for justice to be properly
served, for righteousness to prevail, for fairness.
And then . . .
Watch them shoot you too.

-Olympia Jones

## WHAT YOU'LL FIND A FIVE-YEAR-OLD TASHA DOING IN HER TOYBOX

My friends!
My doll, naked, with a new hair cut
A smear of lipstick and big blue eyes
Just like mine.
My favorite bear
With a missing eye and nearly detached arms.
And a few imaginary pals as well.
This toybox is my airplane, my jeep,
Even my submarine, taking me anywhere
And everywhere at the close of a lid.
Fresh wood, old boogers, and a half eaten bag of Oreos,
That I acquired from a smash and grab
Or is it dine and dash
From the "El Kitchen-O"
My time machine and my space shuttle—
Where shall we go today?
Oh, no, Mom's mad—she is looking for the bag of Oreos.
Hurry! Hurry! I call out my shipmates Doll and Bear!
It's time to embark, and in we go,
With my friends in tow
Whether it's visiting the Smurfs
Punky Brewster or Mr. Belvedere
I'm always safe and sound
In my toybox I could always be found.

-Tasha Roberts

## WHAT YOU FIND AT MY SAFE SPACE

When times are dark and I gotta be safe. I go to the crawl space under our porch. Barely big enough for a six-year-old to wiggle through. When I go inside, I find my blankie, flashlight, open cans of Spaghetti O's, my favorite teddy, knife, sister's binky. Once inside you smell old rust, moldy dirt, stank air, even urine. As I lay there I hear screaming from above, footsteps, wind that sounds like a whisper, things crawling, crickets, the taste in my mouth is like dirty socks. This is my safe place, no one will get me, no one knows where I'd go even for a night they wouldn't know I'm gone. I'm safe in my crawl space 'til dawn. Even as I sat on the moist dirt with my arms on my legs, I know this was my safe place so even in the darkness, I was able to know I was safe in my hole.

-Cyndie Jones

## ODE TO GEESE

They spread their great wings
Soaring free across the sky
Here they come across the fence
They come in to share with us their time.
They grace us with their presence
Their beauty and their peace.

Though they come and go
Though we can't go; together,
We will spend the time behind the fence
Spreading our wings and our peace
With the geese.

-Jacky Scott

## MY GRANDMOTHER'S SHEETCAKE
*(read slowly and sensuously)*

2 sticks unsalted butter
3 heaping tablespoons powdered cocoa
1 teaspoon vanilla
1 cup water
Slow simmer—set aside after hot

Separate bowl

2 cups sugar
2 cups flour
1 teaspoon baking soda
1 teaspoon cinnamon
Dash of salt

Separate bowl

½ cup buttermilk
2 eggs

Add hot mix to dry. Mix quickly while mixer is
On high . . .

Add to greased and floured
Sheet cake pan
For 20 minutes at 425°

Frosting . . . next week

-Lisa Black

## WHAT IT'S LIKE TO BE ME
## (FOR THOSE OF YOU WHO AREN'T)

What it's like to be a single black divorced female
There's a mother on the same yard
With the one who testified against me,
That somewhat has the same bloodstream...
But forgiving, the church lady as forgiven,
From others seeking forgiveness.
Blessed in so many ways.
Raised by a faultless God accompanied by the One
Whose footprints in the sand are
Significant in saving me...
From oceans deep.

What it's like to be someone like me who struggled to breathe,
Who believed she was nothing
But He sent his Son because
He thought I was something.
A heavenly war has broken out and demons scream,
As they are slain... reaching for my soul.
Someone who's a target for persecution and curses,
Mainly by people in the churches,
Let truth be told,
It's real cold,
But I'm not alone.
I have to remember to look above it.
Who can I trust?
'Cause I am sick of it!

What it is like to be me, away from
The three that I bore,
Feeling their pain on top of my pain.
An embrace of the rain.
In a point of time my incarceration locked them up,
Lacerations for our iniquity,
But He still. . . got. . . up!
As He rose, so. . . have. . . I.
My children are a part of me and I in Him.
From the ashes of the dust we. . . will. . . rise.
There are moments I'm stronger, and days
That I ask to lay a fleece. . .
Then there are the thoughts of what life
My kids' dad would have had. . .
Rest in peace.
What it's like to be me.

-Sharee Asberry

## WHAT IT'S LIKE TO BE AN ALCOHOLIC MOM

In this sea of grey
I see tidal waves of pain
Facing the booze soaked monster
And knowing
I am my worst enemy.
Feeling the need to be normal
In a chaotic
Whisky filled brain.
Missing out on wonderful moments,
And the cry and tears.
Getting over the disgrace
But always swallowing the disgust.
Gaining strength from my children's hugs
And them guaranteeing my ending
Isn't written yet.
And realizing it's not about getting sober
But staying sober.
Never doubting I will always be an alcoholic mom
And that soon is only a second away.

-Melissa Rocha

## I CAN HEAR

I can hear you at birth
I can hear you coming home from school
I can hear you when you graduate
And now that you are gone
I can still hear you

-Isabel Garcia

## WHAT IT'S LIKE TO BE A CATERPILLAR

It's like reminding others that you're like a slug with legs
It's crawling around in your addiction.
It's wishing you were someone else, anyone else.
It's watching the blur of the world as it goes on around you, without you.
It's thinking how you'll never be like that caterpillar in Alice in Wonderland,
Sitting all smug like,
Smoking your hookah.
It's suddenly being imprisoned inside of a cocoon.
It's wondering how much of the world is changing around you.
It's dying to know if you'll ever get out.
Finally, you see a sliver of light,
A glimpse of hope.
You feel, I don't know, different somehow.
I feel so crowded, inside my cocoon
I feel different.
I have this urge, this overwhelming desire
To fly, to soar above life's limitations.
Oh, look, that sliver of light is bigger now.
I think I can almost fit through.
What's this? A wing?
Oh wait, now there's two. . .

-Tasha Roberts

## DEAR ISABEL

Growing up was a learning experience. As a kid we played Hopscotch, we jumped rope, played with jacks, cut paper to make paper dolls. We had crawling and walking dolls, made bracelets and necklaces out of beads, talked into two cans attached to a string, played with marbles, road bikes, had slingshots to kill birds, got married.

How I would have loved to treasure all the simple stuff in life, because nowadays we don't have Hopscotch, we just drink the Scotch. We don't jump rope, we use it as a noose. We don't play jacks, we carjack. We don't cut out paper to make paper dolls, we just smoke the paper. We don't have crawling and walking dolls, we have real babies. We don't make beaded bracelets and necklaces, we now have real jewelry. We don't talk into cans, we have cell phones.

How I would have loved to treasure all the simple stuff.

We don't play marbles, we have video games. We don't ride bikes, we have hoverboards. We don't have slingshots to kill birds, we have guns to kill people. We don't get married, we live together.

How I would love to treasure this simple stuff. But, you know what, I did treasure all the simple stuff or I wouldn't have written about it.

-Isabel Garcia

## ODE TO PERFUME

All this assault to
Olfactory senses.
Never again will Chanel
Be taken for granted.
Scents carried on a breeze
Residual vanity to envy.
Patchouli nostalgia
Lingering vanilla
Whispers of spice, musk
The allure of a person
Magnified regardless of appearances
Passed the reck of
Desperation
Regret
Shame.
A magazine sample
Credited to Cosmos
Becomes coveted nearly beyond price.

-Krystal Everett

## WHAT IT'S LIKE TO BE A ONE LEGGED WONDER

What it's like to be a one legged wonder.
Well, it takes a great sense of humor.
You have to be able to make fun of yourself,
cause everyone else will be making fun of you.
You have to be stubborn and have a will of iron
to do the things people tell you that you can't.
People will stare, and you'll have to tell your story
so many times you'll wish you had it in
a pamphlet to hand out.
Kids can be cruel, adults can be stupid.
But you just have to let it go.
Losing your leg at six, gives you plenty of years
to get used to it.
And having a dad missing one too,
makes it that much easier.
But being the one legged wonder means,
goofy stories about legs falling off,
scaring children,
a surprising party trick,
and me being glad it's called a foot fetish,
instead of a feet fetish.
It's learning to laugh and say,
"I may only have one leg, but it's nice."

-Brandi Milligan

## WHEN MY LITTLE SISTER ASKS

Beloved,
I'm in
The place where so called society ends,
And the devil's playground begins, where
Community's rejects, unwanteds, and derelicts reign.

I have no friends, and for that I'm grateful.

The walls—impenetrably translucent, so thick
and clear that they block out the real air.
Sealing in the stench of fear—of what's in your meal,
of stealing a soul, of steeling your once tender now rendered
useless heart, of being apart from you and your nephew.
A stench so full of frightful poison, anger, negativity,
jealousy, ignorance, hatred. Fake phone too much bologna.
Screw everyone, even the "homies."

A place that implants hatred, or amplifies it for you.

I've always disliked thick skin. Now I abhor it.
I'm in a place where I miss my softness because
Humanity and sensitivity are not required here.
The most base desires determines what this created society holds dear.

A place where you are called a towel-headed wookie
and a capital B-witch and where for some dumb reason
beyond my perception everyone calls each other
n*gga, and you get further chewed for calling unarmed cops guards.

And all this is on a good day, Beloved.

On a bad day, this is a place in which you
reside in an un air-conditioned
room with 29 females so that you can watch
other females come out of S.H.U. program
for alleged sodomy or alleged assault with intent
and get cooled semi-private cells.

This is a place where you are liable to walk in
on your cellmate shooting up,
not realizing, in your terrific shock,
that she's gotten high by selling your belongings.

This is a place where you just get told, oh well, too bad,
even if you threaten to beat your junkie cellmate
with a pad lock in a sock while she's asleep.
"Oh well, don't go to prison," they tell you.

This is a place where when you get attacked,
you get punished for it.

So heed my words, my Beloved.

Don't look up to me, but learn well, little girl.
Stay where you are, and God willing, I'll come meet you all soon.

-Olympia Jones

**YET**

I am a number
Counted 11 times a day.

Flashlight to the face at 3 am.
Thanks, I don't need REM sleep
After all.
      No, I'm not dead.
      Yet.

10 am.
How can you lose me at work, officer?
Everyone knows that I work.
Everyone knows where I work.
Everyone knows I only miss work
      For writing class.
I don't even go to Medical
Unless I'm hacking up a piece of lung.
      No I'm not dead.
      Yet.

Of course I got on the count sheet!
I've been doing this for 20 years—
That's at least 16 more than you.
Which of us do you think fucked up?

Institutional recount.

(I am a number
Counted 12 times today.)

Back to work;
Finish the day;
Came home for a "family" moment
With my crew.
Only a moment, then—

Count time.

I'm a small box on that piece of paper
        In the sheet protector
          On your clipboard
Erroneously crossed out
With a China marker.
I'm no more than that
        Not to them,
               Not to you.

But,
No, I'm not dead.
Yet.

-Jax

www.ingramcontent.com/pod-product-compliance
Lightning Source LLC
Chambersburg PA
CBHW062113290426
44110CB00023B/2803